THIS WALKER BOOK BELONGS TO:

_____

_____

_____

_____

For Carolyn Dinan

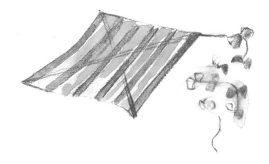

First published 1986 by Walker Books Ltd
Walker House, 87 Vauxhall Walk, London SE11 5HJ

This edition published 1988

Text © 1986 Pamela Zinnemann-Hope
Illustrations © 1986 Kady MacDonald Denton

Printed in Spain by Cayfosa, Barcelona

British Library Cataloguing in Publication Data
Zinnemann-Hope, Pamela
Time for bed Ned.
I. Title   II. Denton, Kady MacDonald
823'.914[J]   PZ7
ISBN 0-7445-0945-9

Time for bed
NED

Written by Pam Zinnemann-Hope

Illustrated by Kady MacDonald Denton

WALKER BOOKS
LONDON

"Ned."

"Time for bed, Ned."

"Oh no!" Ned said.

"Ned!

Bed, I said."

"No. Not bed."

"Come on, Ned."

"Away we go."

"Go! Go!

"Bath and bed," Mum said.

"Splash in the bath," said Ned.

"Into bed, Ned."

"Good night, Mum," Ned said.

MORE WALKER PAPERBACKS

BABIES' FIRST BOOKS

Jan Ormerod
Baby Books

READING   SLEEPING

DAD'S BACK   MESSY BABY

PICTURE BOOKS
For The Very Young

Helen Oxenbury
Pippo

No. 1 TOM & PIPPO READ A STORY

No. 2 TOM & PIPPO MAKE A MESS

No. 3 TOM & PIPPO GO FOR A WALK

No. 4 TOM & PIPPO AND THE
    WASHING MACHINE

No. 5 TOM & PIPPO GO SHOPPING

No. 6 TOM & PIPPO'S DAY

No. 7 TOM & PIPPO IN THE GARDEN

No. 8 TOM & PIPPO SEE THE MOON

LEARNING FOR FUN
The Pre-School Years

Shirley Hughes
Nursery Collection

NOISY

COLOURS

BATHWATER'S HOT

ALL SHAPES AND SIZES

TWO SHOES, NEW SHOES

WHEN WE WENT TO THE PARK

John Burningham
Concept Books

COLOURS   ALPHABET

OPPOSITES   NUMBERS

Philippe Dupasquier
Busy Places

THE GARAGE   THE AIRPORT

THE BUILDING SITE

THE FACTORY   THE HARBOUR

THE RAILWAY STATION

Tony Wells   Puzzle Books

PUZZLE DOUBLES

ALLSORTS